WHAT ARE HABITATS & BIOMES?

LOUISE SPILSBURY

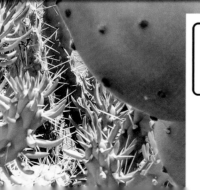

Britannica
Educational Publishing

IN ASSOCIATION WITH

ROSEN
EDUCATIONAL SERVICES

Published in 2014 by Britannica Educational Publishing (a trademark of Encyclopædia Britannica, Inc.) in association with The Rosen Publishing Group, Inc.
29 East 21st Street, New York, NY 10010

Distributed exclusively by Rosen Publishing.
To see additional Britannica Educational Publishing titles, go to rosenpublishing.com

First Edition

Britannica Educational Publishing
J.E. Luebering: Director, Core Reference Group
Anthony L. Green: Editor, Compton's by Britannica

Rosen Publishing
Hope Lourie Killcoyne: Executive Editor
Nelson Sá: Art Director

Library of Congress Cataloging-in-Publication Data

Spilsbury, Louise, author.
What are habitats & biomes?/Louise Spilsbury. — First edition.
    pages cm. — (Let's find out. Life science)
Audience: Grades 3 to 6.
Includes bibliographical references and index.
ISBN 978-1-62275-241-6 (library binding) — ISBN 978-1-62275-244-7 (pbk.) — ISBN 978-1-62275-245-4 (6-pack)
1. Biotic communities—Juvenile literature. 2. Habitat (Ecology)—Juvenile literature. 3. Habitat conservation—Juvenile literature. I. Title. II. Title: What are habitats and biomes.
QH541.14S68275 2014
577.8'2—dc23
                                                                                        2013026792

Manufactured in the United States of America.

Photo credits
Cover: Shutterstock: Pashamba bg, Federico Rostagno fg. Inside: Dreamstime: Aneese 29, Bpperry 20, Dhann05 19, F2 27, Georgeburba 26, Gerardmeuffels 21, Jamenpercy 17, Kuzik 7, Pedro2009 28, Scuba13 9, Sparticus349 18, Zestmarina 16–17; Shutterstock: Jim Agronick 8, Almondd 6, Robyn Butler 23, Chiharu 10–11, Jo Crebbin 22–23, Foxtrot101 14, Antoni Halim 12, Lukas Hejtman 11, Hugh Lansdown 13, LianeM 24, Gerald Marella 15, Pashamba 1bg, Martha Marks 25, Dr. Morley Read 4, 5, Federico Rostagno 1fg.

CONTENTS

Habitats and Biomes

A habitat is the place where a particular group of plants and animals live. Habitats provide living things with everything they need to survive, such as water, shelter, and food.

Habitats can be very small, such as a leaf, or large, such as a forest. Most habitats are smaller than biomes.

A habitat can be as small as a leaf on a bush.

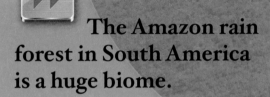

The Amazon rain forest in South America is a huge biome.

A biome is a large area with a certain type of climate. Climate is the usual pattern of weather found in a place. For example, deserts have a hot, dry climate. Biomes have similar weather, so they also have similar plants and animals. Biomes include oceans, rain forests, grasslands, and deserts. Each biome can include many different habitats.

COMPARE AND CONTRAST
What are the similarities and differences between biomes and habitats?

Adaptations

Different habitats and biomes have different conditions. These include various things, such as how hot or cold it is, whether it is wet or dry, and whether the ground is made up of soil, sand, or rock. The plants and animals living in a habitat have special features that help them live there. These features are called adaptations.

An octopus can change color to help it hide on the ocean floor.

Adaptations are special features that help an animal survive in its habitat.

This mountain plant's leaves do not drop off when they die. They stay on the plant, to help keep it warm.

Some plants have adaptations that help them live on mountains, where it is cold and windy. Others have adaptations to help them live in ponds and lakes. Most birds have wings to fly, but a penguin's wings are adapted for swimming. Most living things have adaptations that help them survive in one or two types of habitat. They would not survive in others.

Oceans

Oceans and seas cover almost three-quarters of our planet. Few plants live in deep seas. Near the coast, there are plantlike seaweeds. Seawater is salty and salt kills most plants, but seaweed leaves have a thick coating that protects them from the salt. Seaweeds need light to make food. Some seaweeds have leaves that float to the surface to reach the light.

Kelp

Kelp, a kind of seaweed, grows very tall, so its leaves can reach the light.

Flipper

▶▶ **Dolphins have flippers to steer as they swim in oceans.**

Echolocation is a way of figuring out where things are by bouncing echoes off them.

Ocean animals are adapted to live at sea. Fish have gills that allow them to breathe underwater. Dolphins come to the surface to breathe air. In deep, dark water, dolphins use echolocation to find food. They make clicking noises, and then figure out where fish are from the echoes.

Rivers, Ponds, and Lakes

Rivers, ponds, and lakes contain freshwater, which is not salty. Like all plants, those that grow in freshwater must reach the light. Plants such as sedges and irises grow by the water's edge. They have stiff stems to hold up their leaves. Lilies have long stems that hold their leaves up to the water's surface.

THINK ABOUT IT
River water can move quickly. How might this explain why some river plants have long, thin leaves?

▶▶ A water lily's flat, rounded leaves float like rafts.

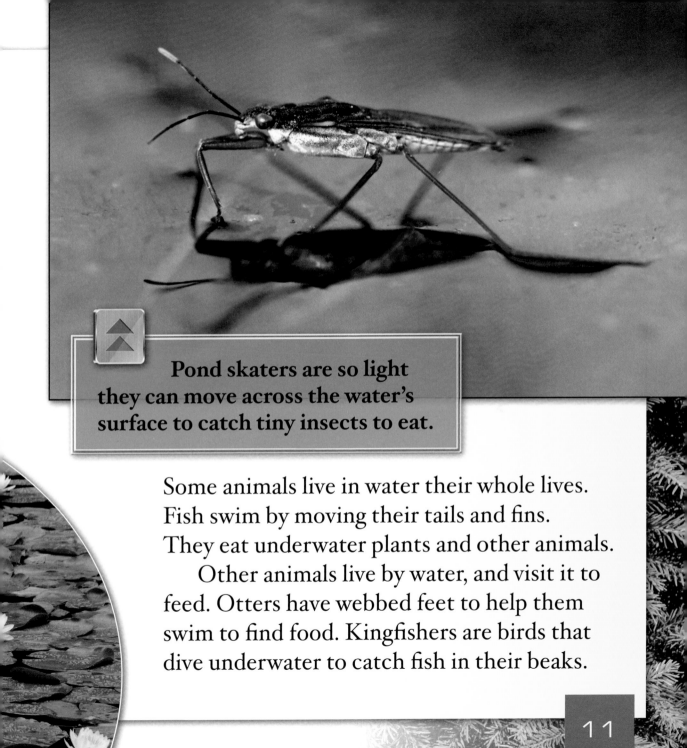

Pond skaters are so light they can move across the water's surface to catch tiny insects to eat.

Some animals live in water their whole lives. Fish swim by moving their tails and fins. They eat underwater plants and other animals.

Other animals live by water, and visit it to feed. Otters have webbed feet to help them swim to find food. Kingfishers are birds that dive underwater to catch fish in their beaks.

Wetlands

Wetlands are areas of land that are very wet for most of the time. Swamps and marshes are wetlands.

Plants that grow in wetlands have many roots, to anchor themselves in the soggy ground. Rice can grow only if its roots are in marshy ground, so farmers build walls to hold water in rice fields.

A swamp cypress has many roots that trap mud so the tree can stand up.

COMPARE AND CONTRAST
How are swamp cypress tree roots and lily roots the same? How are they different?

Fin

Mudskippers use their front fins to walk across mud when the water dries up.

Wetlands sometimes dry up. Mudskippers have developed special features to cope with this. Like all other fishes, they have gills so they can breathe underwater. However, when the water dries up, their gills can carry a supply of air. This allows mudskippers to breathe on land.

WOODLANDS

Woodlands grow in places with warm, wet springs and summers, and cold, dry falls and winters. The maple, oak, and beech trees that grow in woodlands are deciduous. They change with the seasons. In fall, they lose their leaves. This stops the cold from damaging them. The trees rest in winter and grow new leaves in spring.

Deciduous trees lose all their wide, flat leaves in the fall.

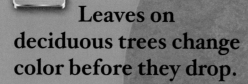

Leaves on deciduous trees change color before they drop.

Woodpeckers break holes in tree bark to feed on wood-eating beetles.

Woodland trees provide food and shelter for many animals. Worms and beetles live on and eat rotting leaves on the woodland floor. Badgers dig homes between the tree roots. They come out at night to eat worms and slugs. Mice nibble seeds and berries that fall from trees. Birds make nests in the trees, and eat berries and insects that live in the bark and branches.

CONIFER FORESTS

Forests of conifer trees grow in places with long, cold winters. Conifer trees have dark green leaves that are long and thin, like needles. Pine, spruce, and fir are conifer trees. Conifer trees have leaves all year round, so they are also called evergreen.

COMPARE AND CONTRAST
How are the trees in conifer forests the same as deciduous trees? How are they different?

▶▶ Conifer leaves are covered with a thin layer of wax that protects them from the cold.

Some animals are adapted to live in conifer forests. Pine sawflies lay their eggs inside pine needles. The young that hatch eat the leaves. Ants make nests from piles of old pine needles. The lynx has a thick fur coat to keep it warm while it hunts rabbits.

▶▶

Lynx have furry feet to stop them from slipping in the snow. They spread out their toes, which act like snowshoes to help the animal walk in soft snow.

Rain Forests

Rain forests grow where it is hot and rains almost every day. These are ideal conditions for plants to grow, so trees here can be very tall. Because of their moist climate, rain forests support more kinds of life than any other habitat.

Rain forest trees have wide roots that grow partly above the ground.

THINK ABOUT IT
How do you think a rain forest tree's big roots help to hold it up?

There are thousands of different animals in the rain forest. Tree frogs drink from pools of rainwater that collect in giant leaves. Monkeys have long arms and fingers. These help the animals grip branches, so they can move easily through the trees to find fruit to eat. Birds, such as the colorful toucan, have big, hard beaks. They use their beaks to crack open and eat rain forest nuts.

▶▶ Spider monkeys have very long arms and a tail for swinging through trees.

DESERTS

When people think of a desert, they usually think of a sandy, hot, and dry place. But there are other kinds of deserts as well. A desert is any large region that gets very little rain each year. These are difficult habitats for plants to live in. Cactus plants have thick stems that store water when it does rain. Desert grasses have very long roots, which spread out below the surface, to help them absorb the small amount of water that is available.

▶▶ Cactus stems have spikes to stop desert animals from drinking the water inside them.

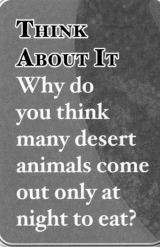

THINK ABOUT IT
Why do you think many desert animals come out only at night to eat?

Scorpions eat spiders, mice, and lizards. They crush prey with their claws, or sting them with their tails.

Many desert animals never drink. Instead, they get the water they need from plants or plant seeds that contain a lot of water. Gerbils eat seeds, and they live under rocks or burrow under sand. Fennec foxes live underground, too, and come out at night to feed.

Grasslands

Grasslands are places where the weather is too dry and the soil too poor for many different types of plants to grow. The land is covered mainly in grasses. Tropical grasslands grow close to the equator. Temperate grasslands grow in regions farther from the equator.

Grasses are tough plants. Their roots lie just below the surface, to catch any rain that falls. Their leaves grow back very quickly if animals eat them. American grasslands are known as prairies.

Tropical grasslands are often called savannas.

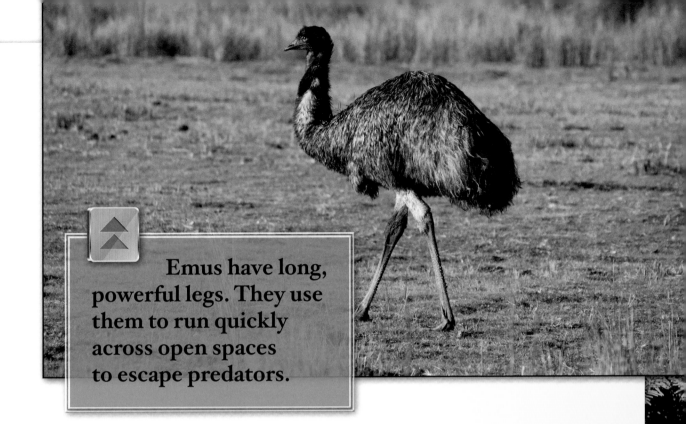

Emus have long, powerful legs. They use them to run quickly across open spaces to escape predators.

THINK ABOUT IT
Why do grazing animals live in herds? How could this help them to spot predators?

Many grassland animals feed on the grass. Prairie dogs eat grass, and then scurry into underground holes to escape eagles. Grazing animals, such as zebras and antelope, live in groups called herds. They are hunted by lions and cheetahs.

SCRUBLANDS

Scrublands are hot and dry in summer, but cool and wet winter. Small trees and bushy plants with woody stems, such as rosemary and lavender, grow here. These plants also have tough, leathery leaves that hold a lot of water. Some plants also have thorns or strong-smelling oils to stop animals from eating them.

THINK ABOUT IT
Why do you think some scrubland plants are adapted to grow back very quickly after fires?

▶▶ Many scrubland plants grow and flower after it rains in spring.

Jackrabbits keep cool by losing body heat from their huge ears.

Rodents, such as voles, and insects feed on the seeds and berries of scrubland plants. The animals hide in the low-growing plants as they look for food. Jackrabbits eat mostly grasses. They have furry feet to protect them from the hot ground. Birds, such as crows, fly over scrubland, searching for rodents and rabbits to eat.

TUNDRA

Tundra is land near the Arctic that is covered in ice and snow during winter. In areas of tundra, it is warmer during the short summers, but even then, the soil stays frozen. Some plants live on tundra by growing quickly in summer and dying during winter. Most plants grow low to the ground, to avoid the harsh, cold wind. Many animals come to eat the plants in summer, but leave again before winter.

In the tundra, most plants grow during the summer season.

Polar bears have white fur to **camouflage** them against snow and ice.

Some animals live in the tundra all year. Polar bears dive into icy Arctic seas to catch seals. They have thick fur and a layer of blubber to keep them warm.

Arctic foxes often eat a polar bear's leftovers. In winter, their brown coat turns white to camouflage them, so they can hunt more easily in the snow.

Camouflage is to blend in or hide against the surroundings.

Under Threat

The main threat to habitats and biomes comes from people. For example, people drain wetlands and dig up grasslands to make space for towns, factories, and airports. Pollution damages habitats, too. Rivers become polluted when factory waste or oil runs into them. When animals lose their homes, they have nowhere to live or have young, and no food to eat.

People clear forests for farming and building. This activity destroys the animals' habitats.

COMPARE AND CONTRAST
What are the similarities and differences between the habitats and biomes you have read about in this book?

Some people help habitats and biomes in different ways. They make laws to stop pollution. They plant new trees. In some places, people develop nature preserves or national parks. These special areas of land are protected by law, so that no one can change or harm them.

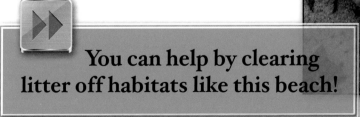

You can help by clearing litter off habitats like this beach!

29

GLOSSARY

Arctic The region around the North Pole.

climate The usual pattern of weather in a place.

conditions The environment surrounding something.

conifer A tree with needlelike leaves. Conifers have leaves all year round.

equator An imaginary circle around Earth equally distant from the North Pole and the South Pole.

fins Thin, flat parts that stick out from the body of a fish that are used in swimming.

flippers The flat parts on the sides of some animals, such as dolphins, that are used in swimming.

gills Body parts used to breathe underwater.

grazing Feeding on growing grass or herbs.

herds Groups of grazing animals, such as zebra or antelope.

insects Small animals such as flies, ants, or beetles.

prairies Grasslands in North America.

predators Animals that hunt other animals for food.

prey An animal hunted for food.

rodents Small animals with sharp front teeth. Rats and mice are rodents.

roots The parts of a plant that grow into the soil.

seeds The parts of a plant made by flowers that can grow into new plants.

shelter Somewhere to stay or live, which protects animals or plants from bad weather and danger.

stems The parts of plants that hold up leaves and flowers.

webbed Skin stretched between fingers and toes.

For More Information

Books

Green, Sandy. *Shelters and Habitats* (Outdoor Explorers). London, UK: Franklin Watts, 2013.

Kalman, Bobbie. *The ABCS of Habitats* (ABCs of the Natural World). New York, NY: Crabtree Publishing, 2007.

Lundgren, Julie K. *Animal Habitat*s (My Science Library). Vero Beach, FL: Rourke Publishing, 2011.

Spilsbury, Louise and Richard. *Habitats* (Young Explorer: Look Inside). Chicago, IL: Raintree, 2013.

Super Nature Encyclopedia. New York, NY: DK Publishing, 2012.

Websites

Due to the changing nature of Internet links, Rosen Publishing has developed an online list of Websites related to the subject of this book. This site is updated regularly. Please use this link to access the list:

http://www.rosenlinks.com/lfo/hab

INDEX